TABLE OF CONTENTS

INTRODUCTION

If 100 children were asked their favorite holiday, they would most likely choose Christmas. Is this also the most loved celebration for parents and children?

This holiday is for many the most stressful and hectic time of the year. This holiday is filled with high expectations and runs on adrenalin, which is what the world wants us to do. Even though we may have the best intentions, it is easy to get caught up in the madness.

This book is a refreshing solution to all the chaos and confusion we've been experiencing. This book is designed to help you and your family have a more meaningful holiday. You will find many tips and suggestions to help you get out of the stress cycle and avoid the financial burdens that over-spending can cause. This book can be used to guide you through creating an environment that focuses on the Spirit of the season. You can choose to embrace it fully or part depending on your family's needs.

Are you ready for a change in your holiday season? From stressful and burdened with debt to joyful and peaceful? This book is for YOU!

PREFACE
My Story

This is my story, and it's the beginning of the greatest idea I've ever had to simplify the holiday. This is one of those ideas you have to try before you dismiss. This idea is one that you must try before you deny. While the rewards and blessings may not be immediate, they are well worth waiting.

My family would not be merry during Christmas 1997. My 12-year marriage ended in divorce on December 4, 1997. It was sad, lonely, and depressing for me and my three daughters. The excitement of my daughters' neighbors was infectious. They fantasized about family parties, building gingerbread houses, decorating Christmas trees, and singing carols at the piano with their families. They tried to conceal their sorrows because they didn't want me to be unhappy. Because they were certain that the truth would not be as loving, they told their friends stories about their Christmas vacation.

Without their father, the home seemed empty. Everything seemed a pale reflection of the holiday. I couldn't make the Christmas spirit seem brighter, and the tree lights didn't shine as brightly. Christmas was about love, and I wasn't feeling loved at the moment. I felt like my heart was broken and I wanted the world stop. I collected my emotions, wrapped them up, and put them away until the end of the yuletide season.

I was a stay-at home mother of three beautiful girls. My part-time income and their father's full-time income enabled our family to have some extras and pay off the debt. The decrease in income has had a negative impact on our family's ability to pay off debt.

In income, I was acutely aware of the fact that this year's hours for opening gifts would be significantly reduced.

I started to think about the best way to start new memories and traditions with my girls, while also keeping in touch with past traditions. I took a class called "How to Bring Christ back into Christmas" one evening in December. The instructor taught us how to decrease the "materialism", which is fueled by lavish gift-giving. She also showed us how to start a new holiday tradition, which she called "The Three Gifts". This system allowed children to focus on receiving gifts while celebrating more memorable holidays such as baking, family time, and celebrating Christ's birth. She believed that toys would eventually lose their charm and expensive devices would become dull. However, sharing time with children, creating memories, and teaching would last the test of time.

I couldn't have received a better philosophy at such a profound time in my own life. I promised myself that I would return home to tell my children the story of Jesus' birth and the beautiful three gifts given by the Three Wise Men. It was a wise idea, and I was eager to see how it would turn out.

This system changed my entire perspective on Christmas and allowed me to see it from a new perspective. My journey and the lessons learned along the way will help you see the Christmas season from a new perspective.

CHAPTER ONE
Are You Constantly in Search of the Perfect Gift?

What makes a perfect gift? We go from shop-to-shop, spending a lot of money, until we find it. Like most people, I would become entangled in the holiday rush and purchase a lot of beautiful packages I thought would make my daughters happy. When I looked back at Christmases past, I realized that no matter how much money we had, there was always something missing. When I realized that I didn't have the money to shop the way I used to in the past, December 1997 was the moment I began to question my motives.

I started to wonder if there was a "perfect" Christmas gift. Is anyone ever able to find it? Is it perfect for the receiver, the giver or both? I was exhausted and stressed just hearing the phrase "the perfect present" made Christmas seem so far away. Is there really just one perfect gift for everyone you love each year?

You might think it is possible to believe that we could find the perfect gift for every person on our wish list if we just had to find one. It is often that when we are trying to find the perfect gift, it becomes two, three, five, and sometimes even more. We plan to start shopping earlier in the year to reduce stress. What we thought was the perfect Christmas gift in July might not be the best in December.

Unfortunately, searching for the perfect gift has become a part of Christmas traditions that is unhealthy. As they watch our madness, our family tradition of giving the perfect gift is passed on to our grandchildren and children.

exhibiting neurotic behaviors during shopping trips. We complain often about how cumbersome it is to shop and spend. It's easy to question whether we are buying what our loved ones and friends want. The thought of them returning gifts they don't like makes us cringe. We start to wonder if all the time spent looking for that perfect gift was a waste of time. To find the perfect gift, we spend a lot of energy and time asking, observing, and conducting secret investigations. Unfortunately, all of our efforts often end in failure. If we asked those who received gifts from us whether they were successful in finding the perfect gift (and we had to be honest), they would most likely answer no.

Let's face it, what we think is the perfect gift might not match the perception of the receiver. Even worse, the gift someone claimed was perfect earlier in the year may change throughout the year. The question is: Why do we keep killing ourselves in this pursuit of perfection? Is there a better way? Why shouldn't we have a different approach to our holidays?

The next chapters will contain easy-to-implement ideas that bring meaning to your holiday celebrations. You will be immersed in the true reason for the season as you implement these ideas and take action.

Today is your chance to make a resolution to improve the way you celebrate Holidays in the future. You can start this year to change the way you think about Christmas. Perhaps the "perfect gift" that you have been searching for is here. Could it be that the tradition is the "perfect gift"? It is true for me and my family. Continue reading.

CHAPTER TWO

How are you Picturing   Christmas?

A planning sheet is something I use whenever I plan a big project for my job, or for my church. I begin to visualize the look I want for the project on paper. I determine the purpose of the project as well as what I want to accomplish. Christmas is no exception.

Let me start by asking you to take some time to write down your thoughts about Christmas in 2011. As an artist uses a brush, to paint his images in his head, imagine how your Christmas will look. Imagine how your family will remember their Christmases as they grow up and celebrate in the future. This will help you to understand your Christmas values. What traditional, visual, spiritual, and mental experiences do you want to create? It's not the right time to have unrealistic expectations about the holiday. Instead, answer this question honestly: "If this were my last Christmas or that of a close friend, where would I put my focus? Or how would it change?"

A great way to get ideas is to make a list called "Christmas without ...”" or ask yourself questions like "What were my most memorable Christmases?" This will help you prioritize and identify the areas you want to be most focused on this year. I encourage you to visit http://threeperfectchristmasgifts.com where you can find this planning sheet where you will find planning sheets to help you with this process. You will also find another planning sheet in the "Reflections” section to help you evaluate the upcoming season. These

Planning sheets are designed to allow you to keep track of all the activities you have done each year, so you can change or repeat them in years to come.

The planning sheets allow us to "Plan with a Purpose", which can be our "theme" for the entire year. Every planning activity must be related to the purpose, and should contribute to it rather than being a distraction. These are the four main areas I recommend as a starting point.

1) The visual appearance of your home

2) Your environment should be conducive to a positive mental attitude

3) Spiritual traditions, experiences

4) Strong presence and importance of rituals and traditions

Each area will be explained in greater detail.

VISUAL APPEARANCES OF THE HOME

Decor in your home sets the mood for the holiday season. It reflects your values and demonstrates what you are most proud of to the people who visit. Every family has different preferences and ideas about how to decorate their home for the holidays. This can make a huge difference to children, and I'd like to share my personal experience.

It was extremely difficult and time-consuming for a single mother to climb on top of her home to hang outdoor Christmas lights. It is a tradition in our area (and perhaps yours) to compete among neighbors for the best decorated home. I have always loved the bright lights in those homes, my daughters.

We were surrounded by them, but they never had the opportunity to see their home decorated in this way. This was true even though I wasn't married.

After my first Christmas as a widow, I asked my husband for his help in decorating our home. My step-daughters revealed that their Christmases were not lit with traditional decorations. This tradition would change the way our family views Christmas. It was hard to describe the feeling of watching our children react as we switched the switch to view our home in harmony with our neighbors. It was a great decision to make the effort to be there for our children in the years to come.

These questions will help you decide how your holiday home should look.

What does Christmas really mean to you? And how can we help others understand it?

What has been the main focus of this holiday in past years (i.e. Santa, Christ,)? What will you do to change the world this year?

Are our decorations simple or extravagant? What message are we trying to convey?

Which mood are we trying to create (love or peace)? How can decor reflect this mood?

What decor will we choose that will continue our family's traditions?

These questions are a great opportunity to involve your entire family in answering them. Planning can be a family tradition. It doesn't have to be complicated or extravagant.

MENTAL ATMOSPHERE IN YOUR SUROUNDINGS

Next, consider the mental environment you want for your family. You will be perceived as calm and collected by your family.

They will become dissatisfied with the season if they are worn out. You can make your home peaceful and eliminate anything that could disturb the peace you want. Your family will feel a sense of peace and joy when you use music, mood and kind words.

SPIRITUAL EXPERIENCES AND TRADITIONS

Your spiritual experiences at home and in your holidays will reflect in the time that you spend teaching the reasons for the season. This is a great opportunity to share your spiritual knowledge and beliefs. Christians should teach about Jesus Christ and his qualities, as well as His example of service. No matter what your beliefs are, this is the best time to instill them into the family's memories.

Let me share a story that will help you create spiritual experiences in your family. My three daughters were given the opportunity to show my religious beliefs by helping a single mom. One of my dear friends knew her. Although I didn't know her personally, I was aware of her circumstances. We had grown to be very close to her children. According to my understanding, the children lived with their dad full-time. They were allowed occasional visits from their mom. During those visits, the mom did not have enough money to care for or feed them. Because I was a single mother, I was able for a brief moment to be like her. My mother's heart imagined me having my children for a short visit, and that I would want to be able to relax and enjoy the time with them rather than worrying about their physical needs.

Two weeks before Christmas, I decided to use some of our grocery money to bless the woman and her family. We arrived at the mother's apartment in the darkest part of the city and were immediately impressed by her humble living conditions.
We were warmly greeted. The scene when we were welcomed at the door holding grocery bags was something I will always remember. The little boy

was more excited for the peanut butter jar and loaf of bread than any other child. As we loaded the bags into empty fridges and cupboards, I can still see the pride in my daughters eyes. It was worth the sacrifices, the hugs, tears, and smiles. We all learned more about charity, sacrifice, and the pure love Christ.

The "Golden Stocking" is another tradition or spiritual experience that we have incorporated in 1997. It is sometimes referred to by others as the "White Stocking". It's a small stocking that we hang (ours are gold) and we each year write a note to Jesus with our gift for Him. The "gift" can be a goal or a habit that we want to change in His honor. We look back at the gift we received in the previous year and assess how we performed. This brings into focus the reason why we celebrate.

A STRONG PRESENCE FOR TRADITIONS & RITUALS

Last but not least, be aware of the family traditions that are most important to you when planning. Start by deciding the five most important traditions that you want to pass on your children. These traditions can come from your childhood or new ones that you want to start, or they can be a mix of different family members.

My previous marriage had taught me how to plan and set the holiday season's tone. I was also familiar with the traditions that were implemented. Step children meant that I had to make an effort to find out about and implement traditions that were important to them. I found great ideas by simply asking questions. For

For example, I found out that my step-daughter's grandmother loved making homemade caramels. She had been a close friend and had spent lots of time together. It was also a tradition my mom and me shared.

It may seem like you have to rush to the nearest craft or chain store to make your holiday picture perfect. But don't panic! Don't let this get you down or take your money out of reach. The next chapters will provide suggestions to help you budget your resources for implementing these ideas.

CHAPTER THREE
What is Christmas Really Costing You?

I went from being a wealthy person to living in poverty almost immediately after my divorce in 1997. It was difficult, but it forced me to review my holiday spending habits. I used to be a stay at home mom, so I had the money and time to prepare for the holidays. I was able to shop, sew, and find the perfect items. All my money and time was spent on my children's shelter and food after my divorce. My vacation was taken up caring for my sick children, which left very little time for shopping. We also had very limited money to purchase luxuries because we lived paycheck-to-paycheck. This is when I began to evaluate the true cost of Christmas, regardless of our financial situation.

Once, I heard that it was more important to spend Christmas HOW than what you spend. If we were to be honest, we would all admit that our attention is primarily on the monetary aspect. What is it we spend our money on, and what are the costs associated with our choices? While we love the idea of Christmas spirit lasting all year, many people find that the cost of paying the bills and compounding interest month after month is too much.

Let's take an honest look at the true cost of Christmas. This evaluation should be both informative and helpful in helping you to make changes to your holiday spending.

Joel Walfogel's book "Scroogenomics"1 states that 2007 was the year of the holiday retail sales.

The Christmas season was worth $66 billion. It would shock you to learn that the average American family spent $866 on Christmas, with an increase each year. Walfgoel explains that when the recipient of the gift was asked their opinion about the gift's value, they most often gave a guess at 25 cents per dollar. Unfortunately, many people go into debt during Christmas, incurring late fees and interest to buy something they don't want or less valuable. This doesn't seem like a financially responsible decision. We do it every year.

Do you fall into the "average household" category?

Or are you like many others who don't know the total cost of Christmas? Whatever your situation, I'd like to share what I did to stop spending too much during the holidays. First, create a budget. Then, set up a system that documents your Christmas outgoings. It is very user-friendly, but it is a good idea. A system will be a key component that will prevent you from getting frustrated, quitting or falling back into old habits. The system that I developed will help you better understand what I mean.

THE SYSTEM

My solution to my outrageous holiday spending was to simplify and organise as a single mother. I created the "Making Christmas Memorable Planning Guide" during those difficult times when I was trying to budget my money properly. The planner comes with printable forms that can easily be saved year after year. Are you an avid smart phone user? No worries! You have a variety of phone apps that can help you track your spending.

Go. To ensure that your information is in one place, I recommend manually recording all purchases in the planner. Click HERE to go to our website and download your "Making Christmas Memorable" planner.
BUDGETING MONEY

Planning a budget requires that you are honest with yourself and be realistic. Don't count income that isn't stable. You must ensure that your spending matches your income. Once you have established a budget, make sure to stick with it.

You may now be concerned that your income isn't sufficient to buy gifts for everyone on your gift list or pay the celebration expenses. It is a good idea to start downsizing (i.e. You can reduce the number of people on your Christmas list from previous years. This is an option if you don't have the budget to spend on Christmas. You can use the following tool for categorizing your list.

Christmas cards Family photos Christmas wardrobes

Christmas baking and meals

Gifts for immediate family members Stocking stuffers and gifts for friends/neighbors

Christmas decorations, lighting and packaging for charitable contributions

Please note: This is not an exhaustive listing. Feel free to add categories that are not included here.

It will be easy to see how much stress and strain you will experience when you plan your Christmas budget and gift list well in advance. Make sure to be very precise when you break down your budget. Also, make sure to note what your budget for each category is and how much you will spend per person (both financially and in time).

BUDGETING TIME

Many people believe that Christmas decorations and gifts are all that cost during the holidays. This is false. Let's answer a few questions. What was your time taken off work to shop? How many lunch breaks did it take to shop online or plan celebration details? What number of meals and how much time did you spend with your family to accommodate the holiday's demands? We may discover that losing valuable time can be just as expensive as losing money if we are honest about our assessment.

It will bring you more peace and harmony at work and at home. Properly managing our time will help us avoid energy-draining tasks like waiting in traffic or shopping at overcrowded malls, picking up last-minute gifts and so on. This season is not meant to drain our cup, but to fill our hearts with the generosity of Christ and love of Christ.

SAVINGS FOR A HOLIDAY

Planning for holiday spending involves both budgeting for Christmas and saving money throughout the year. You can do this by adding a "Christmas category" to your budget.

You won't have to depend on an end of the year bonus or feel stressed if you set aside money every month. If you don't know where Christmas can be fit into your budget, it could be a sign that you are living beyond your means. I suggest that you reevaluate your monthly savings for the holiday, and make it a monthly habit. Christmas isn't an unanticipated event. Christmas comes year after year. It is not necessary to be shocked by your family's budget.

Review your Christmas season for the next five minutes and consider what price you paid. What was I missing? What can I do to make my life easier? These reflections can be written down on the sheet that we created for you. It is located in our "Making Christmas Memorable" planner, which you may already have downloaded from our site. Click HERE if you don't have the planner yet. As a reminder for next year, keep it safe and easily accessible. What next, now that you have a budget in place?

CHAPTER FOUR

*Can I have Perfect, Simple and Meaningful Gifts and
Where do I Start?*

This means you are open to making a change in how you spend holidays. Change is possible only when you make a decision. Make a decision now to make this the year you have a different holiday season. You may not think of Christmas depending on the date you found this book. But, planning is key. This chapter will introduce "Three Perfect Gifts", a tradition that will help you achieve the changes you desire. This "tradition" may be a way for me and my family have a different Christmas. Based on my own experience, I can tell you that it can.

This tradition has been shared with many of my family members, friends, and co-workers, as well as with new people each year. They often ask, "Can I tell you about the three gifts you share with your family?" It was something I heard you say, but I believe that it is important to start the tradition for everyone. Some people are trying to simplify the holiday. Some people are so tight on their finances that they seek ways to reduce expenses. Many are tired of the chaos of the holidays and want to restore religious and spiritual meaning to their homes and lives. It will be a lasting memory for you once you have heard the idea. You will be able to share this idea with your family when the time is right.

Before I tell you all about the tradition, let me share some testimonies from a co-worker and his wife about the "Three Perfect Gifts". The couple just became parents, and they were smart enough start it now. It was wonderful.

Their infant daughter will start the Christmas tradition as a new Christmas tradition. The three gifts were their first year. Steve was asked why they started this tradition.

"To make Christmas more about Christ, and to eliminate all commercialism. This seemed like a great family tradition. It was refreshing to see a purpose behind each gift, rather than just giving lots of gifts. This placed Christ at the heart of the holiday season, and didn't get lost in mall shopping. "

Wendy, his wife, responded with the following:

It was easier to shop and bring more Christ-centered meanings to Christmas. Because I only had a handful of items, shopping took less time. It was also clear that I wasn't buying frivolous items just to fill my tree. Every item served a purpose, and each gift felt more meaningful.

She concluded,

"My favorite part was the "Instead of traffic jams, shopping malls and crowds, we stayed at home to read scriptures, sing Christmas songs, and watch holiday movies. It was much more relaxing and it opened my eyes to the true meaning of Christmas. I was thinking a lot about Mary, the mother of our Savior, and the sacrifices Christ made later in his life. It was one the most memorable Christmas seasons I've ever experienced.

These are the kinds of testimonials that inspired me to write this tradition so that many families around the world can enjoy the peace and blessings it has brought to my family over the years.

It is important to be open to making the necessary changes. Most often, great change can be compelled only by great need. My strong suggestion:

Find the most pressing need to make a change in your life, and then move forward. Perhaps your relationships or health are being affected by financial or busyness. No matter what your reason may be, the Three Gifts tradition can help you simplify Christmas.

Once you've identified the need, focus your efforts on it and create a plan for how to implement the tradition. It is okay to make gradual changes. This will allow you to test the waters and build trust in your family's ability to make this tradition work. You have an opportunity to improve each year, and Christmas is here every year. Are there challenges that can be matched by these blessings? We will discuss the challenges and solutions in chapter 6. Let me now briefly explain the concept behind "Three Perfect Gifts."

CHAPTER FIVE
What is the Three Perfect Gifts Tradition?

It is important for Christians to tell the Christmas story. Our family had to overcome the challenge of keeping the worldly traditions from distracting from the true meaning and purpose of Christmas, which was for us to worship Jesus.

This book will not be for everyone. While I will explain the deeper meanings of the gifts from this perspective I will also demonstrate how anyone can apply this tradition, regardless of their beliefs. Let me start with a Bible reference.

"And they came into the house and saw the child with Mary his mom, and fell down. They worshipped him, and after they had opened their treasures, presented gifts to him; gold, frankincense and myrrh. "

- Matthew 2:11 KJV

My family learned the "Three Gifts Tradition" by me. I started with the story of Christ's birth. Highlighting the section where the Three Wisemen arrive from faraway land to bring three gifts, I will highlight that part of the story. This gift is meant to honor and worship Jesus. The deeper meanings of these gifts will be revealed to me once I have finished.

THE GIFT OF SILVER

Every family receives a gift that represents the gift of gold. This is the "Gift To Cherish" It is a gift that has great value and a high price.

As time goes by, the value of the gift increases. The gift of gold is sometimes used by families to signify the most expensive item on the wish list or the item that the child desires the most. I prefer to give a "cherished" gift with sentimental value.

This is the gift that they love and remember the most. It may take more thought to give a gift that is more memorable than what they really want.

These are our top five picks for "Gifts to Cherish": It's the gift that doesn't lose value but instead becomes more valuable every year.

1. Keep a journal of their ancestors and family history information.

2. Spiritual Growth products such as scriptures and books or music.

3. Heirlooms

4. Jewelry or jewelry box

5. Let us know if you have any questions.

FRANKINCENSE - THE GIFT OF FRANKINCENSE

Frankincense, a spice, was used in rituals to burn incense in Temples. My family redeemed this gift by giving it something extravagant. This was the "Gift for Fun." These are often the most exciting gifts they receive out of all the gifts.

These are the top five gift options we selected for "Gift for Fun".

1. Day trips and extended vacations.

2. Family outings/Group activities. You will love these ideas, which work for both small and large budgets.

3. Our family often receives the gift they've been waiting for and wishing for every year.

4. You can have fun at home with board games or video games.

5. Personal Season or Fun Pass to a swimming resort or recreational park.

Different traditions are practiced by different families. A gift of frankincense is a gift that draws the recipient closer to God.

THE GIFT OF MYRRH

The gift of Myrrh is the third. This was one of the ointments that was used to heal in Biblical times. It was used to embalm dead people and could have been one of Mary's spices to anoint Jesus' corpse. This gift is used by our family to symbolize the "Gift To Use". These are the most practical gifts of all. These gifts can still be fun and exciting depending on how you present them and what experience you have with the gift.

Here are the five best gift ideas that we've chosen for "Gifts to Use."

1. They love their favorite clothing, whether it's shoes, socks, pajamas or underwear.

2. Tools, electronics and appliances

3. Gift certificates. Our creative ideas about personalizing gift cards will make them even more memorable. There are also ideas to give the gift of "self"

4. Gift cards for food/Gasoline, food storage, 72-hour emergency kits. We have posted the best idea of a neighbor for making these practical gifts so much more fun on our website.

5. You can find items that are related to their hobbies, such as crafts, scrapbooking and golf. We have provided ways to add meaning and thought to the gift, which will increase its significance.

Some families gift Myrrh-related gifts that cover the entire body, such as lotions, bath products or clothing.

A OTHER CREATIVE "THREE-GIFT" IDEAS

Families have come up with many creative ways to gift the gifts over the years. These are some of the examples I've seen:

"Something they want, Something they need and Something to read."

Something of wonder (Fun), Some of usefulness (Use), and Something of meaning (Cherish).

They will appreciate gifts that reflect their heart's desire.

They are looking for something they long for, something that will nourish their bodies, and something that will help them spiritually grow.

This tradition can be linked to the Gifts of the Magi or the biblical story, or it can simply be used to avoid "present overload". It can simplify shopping, reduce costs and equalize gifts. It can also be used to teach humility, thriftiness, or spirituality.

You can decide the purpose, themes and how you want to present the tradition to your family using the three gifts tradition. This holiday ritual will last a lifetime and be treasured by generations to come.

Also, I'd like to share some gift ideas with you from the past, future Christmas gifts and ideas from families that have followed this tradition. You can find these ideas at http://threeperfectchristmasgifts.com. Feel free to leave your feedback on our blog and share your ideas.

How can you present this tradition to your family if they are used to receiving more than three gifts?

CHAPTER SIX
Why only THREE Gifts?

Isn't that what you want as a parent? To give your child a "good Christmas."
As parents, we want to give our children the best Christmas possible.
However, as this book shows, giving your child all they want does not
necessarily mean that they will have a happy and healthy Christmas.

I've witnessed the unwrapping of countless gifts and spent hours wrapping
them. It was fun to see each family member open their gifts. However, I find
my experience richer. This new tradition reduces the emphasis on the cost
and emphasizes the heart, sincerity and thought behind the gifts. The
Christmas Eve gift opening was the moment when the holiday seemed to
reach its peak. The joy, laughter, and celebration can last throughout the
season.

It is an incredible tradition that requires a lot of adjustment. The first few
chapters of my book are dedicated to engaging you with the idea. This will
make you ready to change. It will also help you to feel confident and inspired
to implement the tradition, making it a lasting family tradition. It is important
to communicate it clearly and in a way that your family understands and can
embrace.

This was the way I presented the tradition to my family. My daughters and I
had a candid conversation about the changes that had occurred with the
divorce. I explained to my girls that traditions would be continued just like
they were in previous years. I explained that the idea of three gifts was a
good one.

This is a great opportunity to create new traditions with our children. My children also heard me tell them that I wanted Christmas to be centered around the worship of Jesus Christ. My children should know the story of Jesus Christ's life from birth to his death. I believed that if my children learned about Him and His goodness, they would be able to understand His mission and heal from the loss they have suffered.

My first Christmas following this tradition was not perfect because it was my first Christmas without my husband. Because I couldn't fill the Christmas hole in our home, it was hard to create a holiday mood of joy. Perhaps you have been in a similar situation and decided to start this tradition. Perhaps you are without a family member or have limited finances. No matter what your situation, this tradition can present challenges to traditional patterns of behavior.

In my case, I had no choice but to resist the urge to spoil my children and ask for help from my church or family to make up for my guilt. While this temptation is one that many of us will encounter, it is something we all must resist. However, it is a serious mistake to allow our children to live in the present and try to make up for past mistakes. It was the only way to unite our family as a new little one, to begin this tradition and to bring Christ's spirit into my home to heal our hearts. Today, I am able to say that this tradition has brought us unity and the spirit of the season.

A CRITICAL LOOK

Critics of this book might argue that Christmas is a season where families can spoil children, and they want to enjoy the magic this creates. Some critics may think that cutting down on gifts would result in a reduction in the excitement and fun. I'd respond to these critics by

It is said, "Do what works best to create an atmosphere you desire to create." This tradition is great if you want to shift your focus away from "gifts" and instead create a holiday experience.

This tradition might not be right for you, so I'm not going to lie. Everybody's ideal holiday is different. Families who have exhausted from the rush, panic, stress, exhaustion, and short-tempers are my target audience. Continue reading if you're looking for a peaceful, reflective, and relaxed holiday that can begin as early as December 1.

CHAPTER SEVEN

*What are the Challenges in Implementing
the Tradition?*

What are the challenges in implementing the tradition?

People often ask me about the challenges of implementing this tradition. I've been very detailed in my previous chapters on how to put the tradition of three gifts into practice. But, here, I'll try to show some of these challenges and offer some practical solutions.

SELF CONTROL

My first problem was proving my self-control. In my case, I tried to justify having an extravagant Christmas for my daughters. My children were going through some trauma after the divorce. To distract their attention from the fact that there was no chair at the table, they deserved gifts. My little girls deserved it the most. But, I had to be honest with myself and question my way of thinking. What number of gifts would suffice? These gifts would make Christmas bearable. Do I need more gifts to lessen my stress? Or enhance my financial situation? These questions revealed to me that gifts were being used to alleviate our pain. This realization helped me to return my attention to the tradition of three gifts and realized that I was my worst enemy. This tradition was just what my family needed. Ask yourself hard questions if you are having trouble with self-control. You can find the root cause of your problem and change how you think.

TRADITIONS OF EXPENSIVE GIFTS

Another challenge was dealing with my ingrained mindset of years of giving expensive and abundant gifts. My daughters were not excited to reduce their gift giving to three. It was definitely a difficult adjustment for everyone. When you face this dilemma, be wise and honest about your family's needs and make a decision on when and how to continue the tradition. This transition will be difficult for children who have grown up with hours of wrapping gifts. They need to be supported and guided by a loving parent. You should also be prepared to deal with different levels of difficulty depending on the maturity and age of the adults and children involved. Do not be afraid. Children are stronger than we give them credit for.

FAMILY: "BUY IN"

The third challenge is convincing your children to accept the tradition. It is important to communicate the tradition clearly and give reasons that they can relate to. When trying to sell something to someone, I know that creativity and communication are key. Once you have presented the idea, invite your family to get involved by asking them questions such as, "What can we do as families that would make Christmas more meaningful?" Have fun at planning meetings and incorporate them into daily activities, such as dinner conversations. This will create a sense that your family is involved in the planning process.

FITTING SANTA INTO A PICTURE

The third challenge is how to include Santa in the Three Gifts Tradition. There are many ways to incorporate the three gifts.

There are as many families that receive gifts. The gifts I gave them were their presents. They then received a "back-up" gift from Santa, until they understood Santa fully. Let me tell you a story about how I came up with the idea for the "Back Up Santa" gift.

My dad, when he was a small boy, remembers the year he asked his parents questions about Santa's authenticity. Knowing his doubts and wanting to keep Santa's magic alive in their lives, his parents devised a plan. He was disappointed to discover that he only had a handful of presents when he woke up on Christmas morning. His parents advised him to go outside and look out of the window. He could see the presents in the middle of the snow, all the way to his yard's end. Santa seemed to have lost a few presents in his rush to deliver all of the Christmas gifts on Christmas Eve. My dad was thrilled and remained a believer for at most another year.

This story inspired me, and I decided to save a bigger present for my family's first Christmas with the Three Gift tradition. The secret was revealed to my parents, who were staying with us. On Christmas Eve, my dad told the story of his childhood to the girls. My dad was disappointed by the drastic reduction in gifts this year. I told him that I would signal him to bring the bigger gift to our home and leave it there.

It was true. They came down to see the smaller presents. They tried to smile and be happy, but not to show their disappointment. They played with the presents for a few minutes while I watched. They were looking for more presents and unable to accept that Santa had left.

My dad arrived shortly after me signaling him and he placed the gift on my porch. A few minutes later, he called the children and said, "Girls! I believe Santy Claus (that's what he called Santa), dropped a huge box on your door."

"Come and see!" They were delighted to receive this unexpected gift, and it was also a great way for my dad to revisit a part of his childhood. The "back-up Santa" gift was a wonderful way to help them transition into the smaller Christmas.

My children got married and I have been able to give three gifts to either the married couple or the whole family. My husband and I each receive one gift from my three daughters, which makes three gifts total.

Implementing new things is not without its challenges. This tradition is no exception. The long-term benefits are far greater than the difficulties, so I recommend you give it a shot.

CHAPTER EIGHT
What if my Family isn't the
Traditional Family?

You may also face challenges in implementing this tradition with a blended household. It is crucial to get the entire family on board. This sets the tone. This tradition was a 13-year-old tradition that my daughters and I shared before I met my husband. When we first started dating, I gave his three daughters the gifts and explained our traditions. It was something they were familiar with so it wasn't a new tradition for their first Christmas together. It was an adjustment for my husband and my daughters, as gifts were no longer the main focus of our blended family. The gifts would be practical and more focused on Christ's birth and our family. It was difficult for my husband to adjust, knowing that they would get more extravagant Christmas gifts than their other parent.

It was difficult for me to see my husband's struggle to accept this tradition for his daughters and for himself. I understood that I was asking my husband (much as I am encouraging him) to adjust the traditions he had shared with his daughters. I was so convinced of the benefits of this tradition that I made a strong case for him, citing the positive difference in their worship of Jesus Christ and celebration of the holiday. My husband took that leap of faith to make the change for two reasons. He felt my sincerity in what I believed and had seen with this tradition. He also saw how my daughters felt about exchanging presents and was able to see a difference between our families. He believed in me and that his daughters would feel the same as him.

The make-up of non-traditional families can present a challenge in implementing this tradition because of the multiple children, parent(s), grandparents, aunts, and uncles involved. Motives behind gift giving can vary. It can be as simple as a parent desiring to carry on traditional gift giving they experienced as a child to extravagant where the parent creates a competition to see who can give the most expensive gifts.

Whatever your circumstance may be, the keys here are to both *inform* and *honor.* For example, if you are dealing with an extravagant gift giver, try praising that person for being so generous. Doing this, will set an example for your children on the importance of honoring someone else's values and traditions even when they are not your own. Another good strategy is to inform the other family members of your intentions as far as simplifying and even explain the Three Gifts tradition. You may be surprised to find that this may bring relief to them and their pocketbooks, and inspire them to begin a similar tradition. Let's talk about pocketbooks!

CHAPTER NINE

What are the 10 Most Popular Ways to Cut Back on Holiday Spending?

It is not fun to work the whole year just to pay off what you spent last year for Christmas. No wonder so many dread the holidays. There is no peace in over spending. As a single parent I had to learn this lesson quickly as I already had mounds of debt from my divorce and limited income. During this vital learning period I devised the following "10 popular ways to cut back on spending":

1- **Create a Budget** – Creating a budget and sticking to it will help you save money. So many of us want to take this one time of year to splurge and spoil our children. If you can afford it and that is what makes your family happy, then as I said before, go for it. On the other hand, for those of you who are worried sick about either how to afford gifts or worse, how you will pay back all the debt you've incurred, carrying out the simple discipline of creating an honest and realistic budget can save you from stress and keep you debt free.

2- **Start Saving Early** – It is a simple formula to determine what you will spend on Christmas simply divide by the number of months you have before Christmas. Then include it as a separate category in your family budget and create a separate place or account to store the finance (apart from your regular bill and savings accounts). This is the smart thing to do considering many of us lack the self-discipline we need to avoid spending our designated Christmas money. Remember, depending on your tax return or end-of-year bonuses to cover your expenses is a risky alternative that does not take into consideration emergencies and unexpected bills that can occur during the holiday season. If you will commit to starting early you can avoid much stress and strife. Start Today!

3- **Look for Bargains** – If you are a perennial shopper take advantage of after-season bargains! This is a great way to pick up those stocking stuffers often left until the last minute.

 For example, I would do a lot of my clothes shopping for my girls at Nordstroms. Yes, you heard me correctly. I was able to shop at what may seem to some as a more expensive department store. I was able to shop for next year's summer clothes at the end of summer and just as they were putting out the fall clothes. Trendy clothes may change but classic clothes stay in style. My girls were some of the best dressed kids with name brand clothes because I planned ahead. They also lasted longer than what the less expensive chain stores supplied. Because of the quality of the clothing, the clothing could be passed to the younger sisters. If you train yourselves to shop out of season you can save a great deal of money.

Also, don't be embarrassed to shop thrift stores or garage sales. Many times you will find items that are brand-new or still in their original packages!

4- **Cut Back on Events & Activities** – Rather than running from activity to activity, why not choose two meaningful and memorable activities? This will save on both fuel and cover costs.

5- **Give of Yourself or Your Services** – There were times that I would have preferred a neighbor help me rake leaves for a few hours rather than bring me another holiday treat. Without sounding ungrateful, I loved any kind gesture but there were things that I really needed help with as single mom, and didn't feel comfortable asking .   Who on your list could use your service or has a need that you could supply as a gift. Giving a traditional gift is easier to do but if you are watching your money, the gift of service is a great way to save and also build a relationship with your loved ones.

6- **Don't Shop for Yourself -** It is so tempting to stock up for yourself especially when you find a bargain. The statistics of what people spend on themselves is staggering at Christmas time. We can save a lot if we resist the urge to self-indulge.

7- **Gift Wrap Adds Up** – Bows, bags, boxes and yards of Christmas wrap can get expensive. Here are three ways you can save money on your gift supplies:

1) Take advantage of the discount sales held at the conclusion   of the holiday the year before.
2) Ask for boxes at the stores where you   purchase gifts. Many times these will be free of charge.
3) Shop suppliers who sell gift wrap in large quantities and at wholesale prices.

8-**Stocking Stuffers Add Up Quick** – Do you ever find it hard to fill up those stockings? In years past, I had the tendency to purchase "stocking stuffers" at the last minute, which was the catalyst for much of my overspending. To keep that from happening to you here are some secrets:

Fill the toe with tissue paper or a large piece of fruit or other food item.

Wrap the individual gifts in boxes to take up more room.

If your kids are grown you can make a "family" stocking rather than individual ones.

Purchase inexpensive fun gifts from the dollar store that they would enjoy.

9- **Cut Back On the Food** – Weight gain during the holidays is almost universal. And if we were honest, most of us overstuff ourselves at holiday events leaving us feeling uncomfortable and at times sick. A simple way to cut back without feeling deprived is to cut back on the variety served and the portion sizes. This is a small sacrifice to see big rewards in your bank account.

10- **Spend Time, Not Money** – Regardless of the holiday or even the time of year, families agree that what they remember most is not the money or the gift. Most children and adults do not even recall the gifts they received from three or even two years ago. It is the memories of spending time together that matter most. Spend the most precious resource you have which is time and it will pay huge returns in your relationships.

Our discussion in this chapter has been about saving money. Let's look at how to save on time. In most cases, our time is more available than our bank account.

CHAPTER TEN

What are The 10 Most Popular Time-Saving
Tips For the Holidays?

We know that Christmas is one of the most stressful times of the year for most families and many times that stress falls onto the parent(s). How can you lighten the load so that your valuable time is not spent in vain? Don't you want to know what others are suggesting? I did. I wanted to get out of the "rat race" and find a better solution. As a single parent, my time was already stretched to its limits. Adding a holiday schedule of activities was more than overwhelming. So I began to research ways to reduce and make better use of my time during the holiday rush. Here are the top ten most popular I found.

1- **Creating Accessible Space for Supplies & Planner** – As you begin to gather gifts for the upcoming season, it's a great idea to create a "gift closet". It doesn't have to be an actual closet. It can be any dedicated space, including a shelf, drawer, crawl space or storage box. Just make sure you are able to access it throughout the year. Also, keep your "Making Christmas Memorable" planner in a 3 ring binder and know the exact location. I have researched every internet resource I could find so that I could develop the most comprehensive Christmas planner for all users. If you haven't already, join our mailing list and receive the files for this planner as a downloadable PDF. It contains tips that will apply to the next two chapters of this book with printable forms. Just visit our website by clicking **HERE.**

Most of us keep our decorations for the home and tree in a designated spot. What if you did the same the wrapping, gift bags and boxes? I have created a wrapping station and keep an inventory list of what I have and what I need. I watch for after holiday sales throughout the year and stock up during that time. A wrapping station can be used for all occasions but you may want to set aside a specific area for Christmas wrappings.

2- **Designating Holiday Spending Money** – We mentioned budgeting in the previous chapter. However, just as you would designate a space to put your Christmas supplies, it is good to create a designated place for your Christmas finance. This will avoid confusion or temptation to use it for other things throughout the year. Consider a separate direct deposit or savings account. Some banks and even employers have special accounts you can open called "Christmas Clubs". You may be thinking that you don't enough money to make it worth opening an account. Consider this, if you save your change, unexpected checks and rebates, you will be surprised how quickly it adds up making an account a viable option. If you are still not convinced try using an envelope or a jar.

3- **Get Started Early With A Plan** – This biggest catalyst for stress in our lives is failure to allow ourselves enough time. Here's an example. Just say we have a scheduled appointment on a given day. If we are wise and leave our house in a timely manner arriving at our destination 15 minutes early we tend to be calm and at peace. However, if we procrastinate and leave our house late showing up to an appointment 15 minutes late we tend to be stressed and on edge. Christmas planning is no different.

Since we *know* that Christmas comes every year in December we have an amazing opportunity to have a successful holiday season if we take advantage of the time by planning ahead. Since we also know that planning ahead will greatly reduce the amount of stress, here are a few suggestions. First, start planning as early in the year as possible. Next, make a clear measurable plan, which will keep you on task and will ensure that you will meet your goals. Then, update your plan weekly then daily.

You may ask, "If it is so easy why do few people plan ahead?" This is because some people believe that the time it takes to organize and keep records isn't worth the investment. However, in my experience, taking the time to plan will save you time this year and in the years to come. Yes, you will make an investment of time and effort in the beginning, but the long-term benefits of planning far outweigh the damage done by stress and overspending. Start today.

4- **Downsize Gift Giving and Card Sending** – You would be surprised how many of us are "compulsive gift buyers". Buying gifts for every co-worker and acquaintance (often done on a whim) is both time and money consuming. Here are a few ways you can "downsize" your gift giving which will bring relief to both your pocketbook and schedule.

> .Making a list of those who will be receiving gifts along with your budget in mind allows you to prioritize. If you choose not to do the three gift idea suggested in this book, you may just chose to reduce to a specific number of gifts or dollar amounts.
>
> Give the gifts a repetitious theme so that year after year your family knows what to expect. Some of my friends chose to do these three gifts using the following theme: (1) something they need, (2) something to read and (3) something they want. That is just another version.
>
> Drawing names or a "Secret Santa" theme is a great way to reduce the number of gift purchases.
>
> To avoid the bustling crowds during holiday shopping, consider donating to a worthy cause or sponsoring a needy family on the intended recipient's behalf. This works especially well in

communities where neighbors exchange gifts or plate of food. Sending Christmas cards is a great way to cut back on both time and money spent. The great thing is you are not limited to giving pre-made cards sold at a local drugstore. There are many card-making kits, and e-card websites where you can create and personalize. If you are like me, I am old fashioned and love getting physical Christmas cards and so I found the best way to get is to receive.

Allow me to make a recommendation of a system I have been using for quite a few years. This system, which is called SendOutCards.com allows me to keep a database with my addresses and gives me the option to make my own Christmas card with personal photos. It also allows me to personalize with my handwriting font from the convenience of my computer, iPad or smart phone. This company will print, stuff and send the cards for you. Simply, click **HERE** to experience it for yourself.

5- **Make Shopping Simple AND Fun** – The easiest way to simplify shopping is to avoid getting caught up in the rush! Here are a few ideas to help you accomplish this goal:

Start early and have an accessible list. I know what you are thinking. Lists, lists and more lists. It does take extra time, but is a necessary discipline to avoid frustration, stress and overspending. Another way to make shopping easier and more time efficient is to choose opportunities that have a specific time allowance. For example, lunch breaks at work or a block of time you would normally wait such as a child's activity.

Shopping online can save you hours of commuting and standing in line.

If you plan specific days to doing your Christmas shopping, plan your route so you don't have to backtrack.

Gift cards are often thought of as a last minute gift. However, there are ways to make them personal and fun. They can also be purchased all through the year. It's important to watch expiration dates with gift cards or certificates.

As you are shopping or even baking, have a little extra on hand to give as last minute gifts to neighbors, friends or family members that you may have forgotten or who bring you an unexpected gift. Buying or baking extra saves time from making extra trips to the store.

6- **Calendar Your Holiday Events** – As my family grows and with the busy schedules we all have, I have found that calendaring ahead will allow for better attendance, less hurt feelings and ensures you are fitting in what is most important. Do not over-schedule yourself or those you love. Be sensitive to other family members' demands for work and other family party plans.

Not only can you put holiday events on your calendar, but you can save time by time by calendaring a specific time to mail or deliver gifts so that they can be received in a timely manner. Be sure to calendar activities that are time sensitive such as hand making gifts or sending gifts by mail.

Plan your menus and what goods you will bake ahead of time, detailing their specific ingredients. Add this information to your regular shopping list to avoid several trips to the grocery store.

When it comes to baking if you are pressed for time, don't be afraid to delegate to a local bakery rather than inflict unnecessary stress on yourself.

7- **Plan Travel Far In Advance** –If you have travel for the holidays, plan ahead. Again, start your travel list found in the planner on our website. Get airfare or hotels scheduled ahead of time for better pricing.

8- **Pay Attention to Your Health** – Taking care of your health really does save you time. With good health you are more efficient, less time is spent in bed or in a doctor's office. Remembering to eat healthy and exercise will give you the extra energy that the holiday season demands. Plan healthy meals to accompany all the sweets we normally consume during the holidays. Extra exercise may be needed to avoid having to make a larger New Year's Resolution to get us back into shape. Be aware of how much sleep you are getting. People who are stressed are prone to self-medicate with food, alcohol or drugs. That gives us just one more reason to plan ahead.

9- **Take A Breath** – Taking some time throughout the season to just breathe and enjoy the moment will re-energize you. It will increase your efficiency. Stop to enjoy the beauty of the season.

10– **Communicate Your Plans** – Communicating your holiday plans is vital during the season. Statistics show that the holiday season is a time where many relationships are compromised and many enter into deep depression. Don't let your family become a statistic. If you intend to downsize your gift list or implement the 3 gifts tradition, make sure your family is aware.. Marriages and grandchildren can increase the need for flexibility. Grown children want to start their own traditions so communicating with them about what traditions they would still like to continue with you will be important.

CHAPTER ELEVEN
What do you Hope They Remember?

I mentioned at the beginning of this book that the Christmas season is the holiday which will be most etched in your loved ones memory. What do you want them to remember about the Holiday season? Seldom do those kinds of memories happen year after year without some planning and effort. Both of which are necessary ingredients to creating a "good" Christmas for you and your loved ones.

Create the magical moments of childhood. You can do this if you have saved your resources of both time and money. Take the time to read Christmas stories, watch the traditional movies both new and old, visit Santa, drive around your city and look at the lights, and all the other amazing things we sometimes overlook. If you have communicated with your family from the beginning, you will know what is "magical" and important to each of them.

Make sure you have planned this upcoming holiday with a specific purpose. Was your purpose to spend more time as a family? Perhaps you had planned to start one new tradition. Was your specific goal to teach your children to serve others? All of these are gratifying ways to reach your purpose for celebrating differently this year.

When you put the tree away this year, ask yourself if you were successful. How do you evaluate if your holiday was successful? Ask yourself what were the highlights and what you can improve on for next year. Remember, your very best source of information is your family and loved ones.   When you receive this feedback don't just make a mental note, write it down in your Christmas planner.

May you and your family have a simple, peaceful and beautiful Christmas season and one that fosters love and memories just as vivid as you have imaged. Thank you for allowing me to share our family tradition with you. I am confident that as you implement the tradition of the "Three Gifts" this year, it will make a very profound and lasting impression with your family. Merry Christmas!